# SHOTOKAN KARATE

## 10th kyu to 6th kyu

### Sensei K Enoeda · 8th Dan

A & C Black · London

First published 1996 by
A & C Black (Publishers) Ltd
35 Bedford Row, London WC1R 4JH

Copyright © 1996 by Tiger Corporation

ISBN 0 7136 4311 0

A CIP catalogue record for this book
is available from the British Library.

Printed and bound in Great Britain by
Hillman Printers Ltd, Frome, Somerset

*Acknowledgements*
Written by Jim Lewis 5th Dan.
Thanks to Steve Smith 3rd Dan, Rod
Butler 3rd Dan, Chieko Buck.
Sensei Enoeda's assistants: Sensei Y. Ohta
5th Dan, Sensei J. Lewis 5th Dan.

Back cover photograph by Adrian Nessel.
All other photography by Sylvio Dokov.

*Disclaimer*
Whilst every effort has been made to
ensure accuracy within this book, the
writer and his publisher cannot accept
any responsibility for accident or injury
caused through misinterpretation of its
contents. The reader is urged to use the
book as a complement to regular training
with a qualified instructor.

# Contents

松濤館

# Introduction

To the tens of thousands of students throughout the world who are already practising karate-ka, the names **Shotokan** and **Keinosuke Enoeda** are synonymous.

## A history of Shotokan karate and the Japan Karate Association

The late 1970s and early 1980s saw a great explosion of interest in the martial arts, the effects of which continue to this day. The result is a multitude of styles and organisations, some of which have developed and prospered while others have declined and disappeared. One style which has grown to become one of the most widely taught is Shotokan as practised by the Japan Karate Association (JKA). Formed in 1955, the JKA is now the world's largest Shotokan karate organisation, with affiliated members in almost every country throughout the world. Great Britain is affiliated through the Karate Union of Great Britain (KUGB).

To trace the origin of karate we have to go back over a thousand years to ancient China, to the monastery at Shao Lin. Here the students were taught the art of fighting as part of their spiritual and religious training, and as a way of building strength and character.

These fighting techniques were later imported to Okinawa where the feudal Lord of that time had banned the carrying and use of weapons. These Chinese techniques combined with the local fighting techniques of the islands to form a self-defence fighting system which developed into what we know today as karate.

## Gichin Funakoshi

One master of these fighting arts was **Gichin Funakoshi,** considered to be the founder of the modern day Shotokan style. Originally from the island of Okinawa (where he had studied various forms of martial arts), he first introduced the style to Japan in 1922. There he opened his first dojo (training hall) in 1936. 'Shoto' was his nickname; hence the name **Shoto kan** – Shoto's house or hall.

Master Funakoshi died at the age of 87 in 1957 but not before he had witnessed the inception of what was to produce, through the now famous JKA instructor training programme, some of the finest karate instructors in the world.

# Keinosuke Enoeda

Among that élite group of early instructors was Master Keinosuke Enoeda, the 'Tiger' of whom so much has already been written. Born in 1935 a direct descendant of two Samurai lines, he first began studying judo and attained the rank of second degree Black Belt. At the age of 15 he began studying karate under Master Gichin Funakoshi and Masatoshi Nakayama, who was later to become the Chief Instructor of the JKA.

After graduating from university in 1957, he was invited to enroll on the three-year instructor's course at the JKA. It was during this time that he became All-Japan Champion, earning the nickname 'Tiger' for his exceptional fighting spirit. He is also credited with possessing the strongest punch in all of Japan, a result of his tremendous technique and constant practice on the makiwara (striking board).

On completion of the instructor course, Master Enoeda travelled the world for several years teaching karate, eventually settling in Great Britain. Here he made his home and here he has remained for the past 30 years as the Chief Instructor of the KUGB. It is without doubt that through his unique training and teaching ability, much admired and respected by instructors and students everywhere, Master Enoeda has been a leading figure in making Great Britain one of the strongest karate countries in the world. Master Enoeda continues to teach at his own dojo, and throughout the world where his spirit and dedication to karate are as much a source of inspiration as they were 30 years ago.

Together, the two volumes in the Shotokan karate series will guide the student from beginner right through to Black Belt, with expert guidance, from one of the world's most dynamic karate instructors. I have been a student of Sensei Enoeda for over 25 years, and I was very proud to be asked to contribute to this series which I know will not only delight, but become an invaluable source of reference to all Shotokan karate students whether they are already training or are just about to start.

Both volumes are designed to provide a comprehensive textbook covering each 'grade' (level of advancement) through which the student will be required to progress. However, it must be stressed that no amount of text or number of photographs can compensate for regular training. Only through constant practice will the student become proficient and excel at karate.

If this approach is adopted and a regular training programme adhered to, the rewards will be very worthwhile.

## Karate as exercise

It is worthwhile remembering that karate practice is an ideal way to promote a healthier lifestyle. The exercises involve the use of the whole body, enhancing flexibility, muscle strength and stamina to develop a well balanced body.

Karate can be practised alone or in a class group, it does not require a partner, or any special equipment or apparatus, and can be practised just about anywhere. It is suitable for men and women of all ages, and as a 'kata', for example, takes about two minutes to perform, it does not require a huge amount of time. Regular training can help to build character and discipline as well as self-confidence.

Karate, however, is much more than just physical exercise. Karate requires a positive mental attitude allied with appropriate etiquette, which should be adopted both in and out of the dojo. Always maintain a courteous and respectful attitude not only towards your teacher and fellow students, but also towards everyone you come into contact with.

This positive mental attitude is best illustrated as follows. At the end of each lesson the whole class adopts a kneeling position and after a few moments silence all the students together repeat the following.

**Dojo code** (*See* artwork below.)
- Seek perfection of character.
- Be faithful.
- Endeavour.
- Respect others.
- Refrain from violent behaviour.

These five tenets should form the basis not only of your karate practice, but also your attitude to everyday life. As you progress through your karate training you will begin to realise the importance of a correct mental attitude.

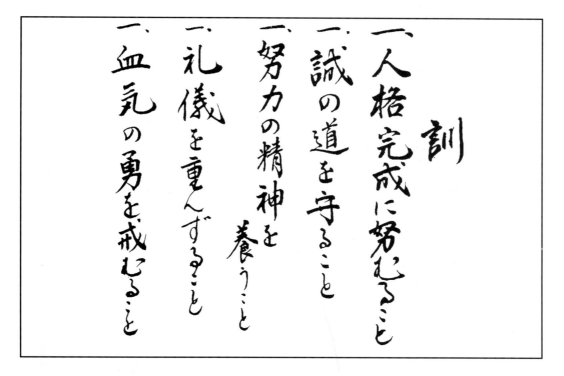

訓
一、人格完成に努むること
一、誠の道を守ること
一、努力の精神を養うこと
一、礼儀を重んずること
一、血気の勇を戒むること

I would like to say a special thank you to Sensei Yoshinabu Ohta, 5th Dan JKA, for all his help in putting together this series and for demonstrating his superb techniques. Sensei Ohta is a graduate of the famous Takushoku University, Japan. He was placed third in kata in the 1986 All-Japan Karate Championships, and has been Sensei Enoeda's assistant since 1982. Without his invaluable aid these books would not have been possible.

Finally, I would like to convey some of my own personal experiences in over 25 years in karate. During that time I have been most fortunate in being taught by some of the finest instructors in the world, some of whom have now become good friends.

Some students who started out with me and are now themselves instructors have also become close personal friends, and have been very helpful in putting together this series. I would like to particularly thank Mr Steve Smith, 3rd Dan, for his invaluable comments and criticisms.

Wherever I have travelled in the world, I have always found a local dojo where I have without exception been made extremely welcome, and where I have met some fascinating and interesting people. One such trip to Thailand in 1988 led me to be appointed the Head Coach to the Thai National Karate Team, representing Thailand at the South East Asian Games in Kualar Lumpar in 1989. Over the years karate has enabled me to be involved in many such opportunities, and I hope that those of you who are starting out on your karate training will find it as rewarding and enriching as I have.

**Jim Lewis 5th Dan**

Master Enoeda's dojo is located at: 16 Marshall Street, London W1V 1LN (tel 0171-734-0900).

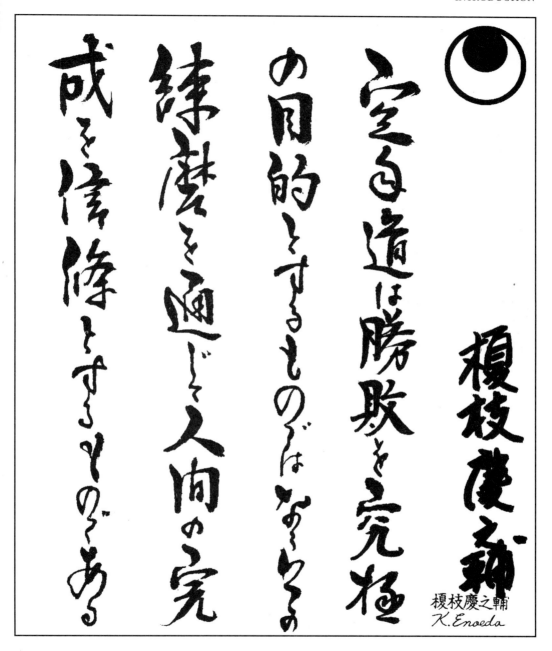

空手道は勝敗を完極の目的とするものではなくその練磨を通じて人間の完成を信條とするものである

榎枝慶之輔
K. Enoeda

*The ultimate aim of the art of karate lies not in victory or defeat, but in the perfection of the characters of its participants.*

**Gichin Funakoshi**

Each book is divided into separate levels for each grade, and each level covers **kihon – kata – kumite.**

### Volume one: 10th kyu to 6th kyu
Level one:    9th kyu
Level two:    8th kyu
Level three: 7th kyu
Level four:   6th kyu

### Volume two: 5th kyu to Black Belt
Level five:    5th kyu
Level six:     4th kyu
Level seven: 3rd kyu
Level eight:  2nd kyu
Level nine:   1st kyu
Level ten:    shodan 1st Dan

# Warm-up

Before you begin your karate practice or any type of strenuous exercise, it is important to thoroughly warm up the whole body through a series of gentle movements and stretches. This prepares the body for the actual karate movements.

# Grading

Shotokan karate has a system of grades or levels of competence (kyu) from 10th kyu (beginner) to 1st kyu. The next level up from 1st kyu is Black Belt or shodan (1st Dan). When a student reaches a certain level of proficiency, he or she may try for a grading (assessment) and if successful the student is entitled to wear a coloured belt which denotes the grade attained. These are:

10th kyu – White Belt
9th kyu  – Orange Belt
8th kyu  – Red Belt
7th kyu  – Yellow Belt
6th kyu  – Green Belt
5th kyu  – Purple Belt
4th kyu  – Purple Belt
3rd kyu  – Brown Belt
2nd kyu  – Brown Belt
1st kyu  – Brown Belt
1st Dan  – Black Belt.

Each grade consists of three elements: **kihon** (basic techniques); **kata**; **kumite** (sparring). Before a student can try for a grade he or she will have to be proficient in all three elements relevant to the grade they are taking.

# Kata

To fully explain all the principles involved in the meaning of kata would take a complete book on its own! This is not the purpose of this series. Much has already been written on the subject of kata; the student would be advised to seek out these publications for a more detailed understanding.

Put in its most simplistic form, kata is a series of pre-arranged movements of defence and attack, performed in a specific sequence against one or more imaginary opponents. In earlier times kata was used as a means of teaching technique. When techniques were shown in pre-arranged sequences they could be remembered and practised.

Kata involves the use of all the techniques found in karate: punch, strike, kick, evade, balance, jump, the correct use of power, speed, co-ordination, breathing and timing. All these elements are used and brought together in kata practice.

Daily practice in kata will not only help the student to improve his or her technique, but will also assist in learning the true meaning of karate.

The Shotokan style as shown in this series has a total of 27 katas. For our purposes, however, this series covers only eight of those required to Black Belt. They are:

(1) kihon
(2) heian shodan
(3) heian nidan
(4) heian sandan
(5) heian yondan
(6) heian godan
(7) tekki shodan
(8) bassai dai.

*Note* Within each of the kata sections the counts are indicated by ❶, ❷, ❸, etc.

# Level one (9th kyu)

## Kihon

**Fig.1** *Zenkutsudachi* (front stance); *Junzuki* (stepping punch). Shows the basic front stance with *Gedanberai* (downward block) moving to stepping punch (*Junzuki*). Keep your front knee bent so that most of your weight is on your front leg. Keep the feet about shoulder width apart. To step forward move your back foot across the floor towards your front foot and step outwards so the feet are again shoulder width apart. The hips and upper body are kept straight.

Side view

**Fig.1**

Side view

**Fig.1**

Side view

**Fig.2** *Ageuki* (rising block). Shows an upper rising block for defence against an attack to the face. The feet move the same way as a stepping punch. The arm makes an upward blocking movement and the hips and upper body are turned to a 45° angle.

Side view

**Fig.2**                                    Side view

**Fig.2**

Side view

**Fig.3** *Sotouke* (outside block). Shows an outside block for defence against an attack to the mid-section. Again the feet move as before with the arm making a downward movement from above the shoulder to a point in front of the chest, making a block with the inside of the forearm.

Side view

**Fig.3**

Side view

**Fig.3**

Side view

**Fig.4** *Uchiuke* (inside block). Shows an inside block also for defence against an attack to the mid-section. The foot movement is the same as before, with the arm making a movement from under the opposite arm to make a block with the outside of the forearm.

Side view

**Fig.4**

Side view

**Fig.4**

Side view

**Fig.5** *Maegeri* (front snap kick). Shows the basic front snap kick. From front stance, lift the knee and make a snap kick by pulling back your kicking foot as fast as possible. Strike with the 'ball' of the foot.

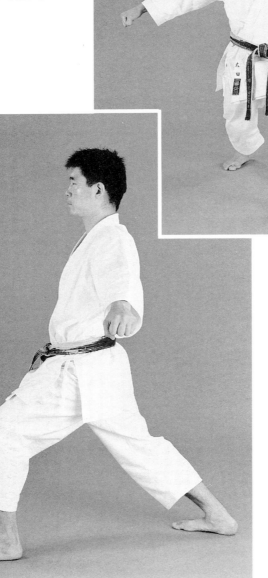

Side view

**Fig.5**

Side view

**Fig.5**

Side view

**Fig.5**

Side view

**Fig.5**

Side view

# Kata: kihon

基本形

**Fig.1** *Yoi* (ready).

**Fig.2** *Gedanbarai* (downward block). Move your left foot to your left side and make a front stance downward block with your left hand.

❶

❷
**Fig.3** *Junzuki* (stepping punch). Make a
stepping punch with your right hand.

**Fig.4** Move your right foot to face the opposite direction and make a downward block with your right hand.

❸

**Fig.5** Make a stepping punch with your left hand. ❹

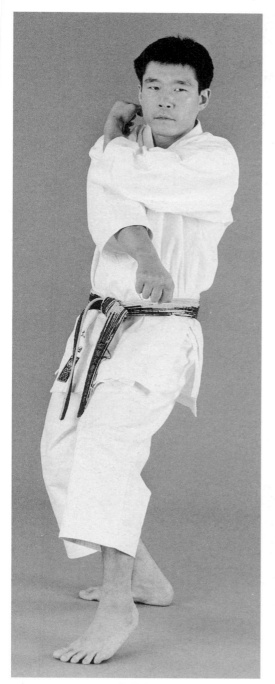

**Fig.6** Move your left foot to your left side and make a downward block with your left hand. ❺

❻
**Fig.7** Make a stepping punch with your right hand.

❼
**Fig.8** Make a stepping punch with your left hand.

**Fig.9** Make a stepping punch with your right hand with *Kiai*. ❽

**Fig.10** Move your left foot, turn to your left side, and make a downward block with your left hand.

❾

❿ **Fig.11** Make a stepping punch with your right hand.

**Fig.12** Move your right foot to the opposite direction and make a downward block with your right hand.

⑪

40

⑫ **Fig.13** Make a stepping punch with your left hand.

**Fig.14** Move your left foot to your left side and make a downward block with your left hand.

Side view

**Fig.15** Make a stepping punch with your right hand.

Side view

**Fig.16** Make a stepping punch with your left hand.

Side view

**Fig.17** Make a stepping punch with your right hand with *Kiai*.

Side view

**Fig.18** Move your left foot to your left side and make a downward block with your left hand.

**⑰**
Side view

⓲ **Fig.19** Make a stepping punch with your left hand.

**Fig.20** Move your right foot to the opposite direction and make a downward block with your right hand.

⑲

**Fig.21** Make a stepping punch with your left hand.

**Fig.22** Move your left foot back to the ready position.

# Application

**Figs 23, 24 and 25** demonstrate the application of figs 4 and 5 from kihon kata.

**Fig.23**

**Fig.24**

**Fig.25**

# Kumite: three-step sparring

Kumite is the practical application of techniques which have been learned by the student from basic training and practice in kata. When you practise kumite, you are face to face with your opponent.

There are different kinds of sparring used in the Shotokan system.

(1) **Sambon kumite**: basic three-step sparring; sometimes five steps are used.
(2) **Kihon ippon**: basic one-step sparring.
(3) **Jiyu ippon**: semi-free one-step sparring.
(2) **Jiyu kumite**: free sparring.

Three-step sparring consists of basic pre-arranged attacks and defence. It is the first type of sparring to be taught. The student will have to be proficient in three-step sparring for Levels one to three (7th kyu).

One-step sparring consists of pre-arranged attacks from a basic position, but with the defender determining the block and counter attack. The student will have to be proficient in one-step sparring for Levels four to eight (3rd kyu).

Semi-free sparring also consists of pre-arranged attacks again with the defender determining the block and counter attack, but with both opponents adopting a 'free style' position. Both opponents are able to move about freely.

Free sparring allows both opponents to move about freely and make any attack or defence. It involves any attack or combination of attacks and any defences using blocking techniques, evading and counter attacking. It requires great skill in timing, speed, power and control. This is required for students taking 1st Dan grading.

After bowing, both opponents assume a ready position. The attacker steps back into front stance.

The attacker then makes a stepping punch to the face, and the defender steps back and makes an upper rising block.

The attacker then makes another stepping punch to the face, with the defender making an upper rising block.

The attacker then makes a third stepping punch to the face and again the defender makes an upper rising block but also counters with a reverse punch (*Gyakuzuki*).

Both attacker and defender step back to ready position and the same sequence is repeated with attacker and defender changing. When these three attacks have been completed, again the opponents step back to ready position.

The first attacker again steps back and makes a stepping punch to the opponent's mid-section with the defender making an outside block. The attacker makes two more punches and after once more stepping back to the ready position, the attacks again change so that both opponents end up at the starting position.

Three-step sparring is for Levels one, two and three.

# Level two (8th kyu)

## Kihon

**Fig.6** *Shutouke* (knife hand block); *Kokutsudachi* (back stance). Shows the position for making a knife hand block and back stance. Keep your weight on to your back leg. When moving, your foot moves across the floor in a straight line. Your hands are open to make a 'knife hand' block or strike with the outside edge of the hand.

Side view

**Fig.6**

Side view

**Fig.6**

Side view

**Fig.7** *Yokokeage* (side snap kick); *Kibadachi* (straddle stance). Shows a side snap kick from a straddle stance position. In this stance your weight is divided equally on both legs. When moving, cross one foot over the other and lift the knee to make a snap kick with the edge of the foot. Pull back your kicking leg as fast as possible.

**Fig.7**

63

**Fig.7**

**Fig.7**

**Fig.8** *Yokokekomi* (side thrust kick). Shows a side thrust kick also from straddle stance position. When moving, cross one foot over the other as in the snap kick. Lift the knee to make a thrust kick with the edge of the foot.

**Fig.8**

**Fig.8**

# Kata: heian shodan

**Fig.1** *Yoi* (ready).

**Fig.2** Move your left foot to your left side and make a front stance downward block with your left hand.

❶

❷

**Fig.3** Make a stepping punch with your right hand.

**Fig.4** Move your right foot to the opposite direction and make a downward block with your right hand. ❸

**Fig.5** *Kentsuiuchi.* Pull both your right hand and right foot back and make a hammer fist strike.

❹

❺
**Fig.6** Make a stepping punch with your left hand.

❻
**Fig.7** Move your left foot to your left side and make a downward block with your left hand.

**Fig.8** *Ageuki*. Step forward and make an upper rising block with your right hand.

**Fig.9** Step forward and make an upper rising block with your left hand. ❽

**Fig.10** Step forward and make an upper rising block with your right hand with *Kiai*. ❾

**Fig.11** Move your left foot to your left side and make a downward block with your left hand.

⑩

⑪

**Fig.12** Make a stepping punch with your right hand.

**Fig.13** Move your right foot to the opposite direction and make a downward block with your right hand.

⑫

⑬

**Fig.14** Make a stepping punch with your left hand.

⑭

**Fig.15** Move your left foot to your left side and make a downward block with your left hand.

⑮

**Fig.16** Make a stepping punch with your right hand.

**Fig.17** Make a stepping punch with your left hand.

**Fig.18** Make a stepping punch with your right hand with *Kiai*.

**Fig.19** *Kokutsu dachi shutouke*. Move your left foot to your left side and make a back stance knife hand block with your left hand.

⑱

**Fig.20** Step with your right foot to a position of 45°, and make a knife hand block with your right hand. ⑲

**Fig.21** Move your right foot to your right side and make a knife hand block with your right hand.

**㉑**

**Fig.22** Step with your left foot to a position of 45°, and make a knife hand block with your left hand.

**Fig.23** Step back with your left foot to assume the ready position.

# Application

**Figs 24, 25 and 26** demonstrate the application of figs 4 and 5.

**Fig.24**

**Fig.25**

**Fig.26**

# Kumite: three-step sparring

As for Level one.

# Level three (7th kyu)

## Kihon

**Figs 9 and 10** *Uraken* (back fist strike). Show a back fist strike from a straddle stance position. Fig.9 shows a back fist strike from a downward angle as in the kata heian sandan. Fig.10 shows a back fist strike using a sideways movement.

**Fig.9**

**Fig.10**

**Fig.10**

**Fig.11** *Nukite* (spear hand strike). Shows a spear hand strike. The fingers are pressed together and thrust forward, keeping them straight. The striking point is the tips of the fingers.

# Kata: heian nidan

**Fig.1** *Yoi* (ready).

**Fig.2** *Haiwanuke*. Move your left foot to your left and make a back stance double hand block.

❶

94

**Fig.3** Left arm: *Nagashiuke;* right arm: *Kentsuiuchi.* Make a block by your left hand. At the same time attack with your right hand.

❷

❸

**Fig.4** *Sokumenzuki.* Make an attack with your left hand to your opponent's mid-section.

**Fig.5** Turn to face the opposite direction and make a double hand block as in fig.2.  ❹

**Fig.6** Make a block with your right hand. At the same time attack with your left hand.

❺

❻

**Fig.7** Make an attack with your right hand to your opponent's mid-section as in fig.4.

**Fig.8** *Urakenuchi yokokeage*. Move your left foot halfway and pull back your right leg. Make a side snap kick and at the same time a back fist strike.

Side view

**Fig.8**

Side view

**Fig.8**

❼

Side view

**Fig.9** *Shutouke*. Step down with your right foot into back stance and make a knife hand block with your left hand.

Side view

101

**Fig.9**

❽

Side view

**Fig.10** Step forward and make a ❾
knife hand block with your right hand.

**Fig.11** Step forward and make a ❿
knife hand block with your left hand.

**Fig.12** Left arm: *Osaeuke*; right arm: *Nukite*. Step forward into front stance. Make a downward pressing block with your left hand and a spear hand attack with your right with *Kiai*.

**Fig.13** Move your left foot to your left side and make a back stance knife hand block with your left hand.

**Fig.14** Step with your right foot to about 45°, and make a knife hand block with your right hand.

**Fig.15** Move your right foot to your right side and make a knife hand block with your right hand.

**Fig.16** Step with your left foot to about 45°, and make a knife hand block with your left hand.

**Fig.17** *Uchiuke* (*Gyakuhanmi*, half *Zenkutsudachi*). Move your left foot to your left and make an inside block with your right hand.

Side view

**Fig.17**

Side view

**Fig.18** *Maegeri*. Make a front snap kick with your right leg.

Side view

110

**Fig.19** Make a reverse punch with your left hand.

Side view

111

**Fig.20** Make an inside block with your left hand.

Side view

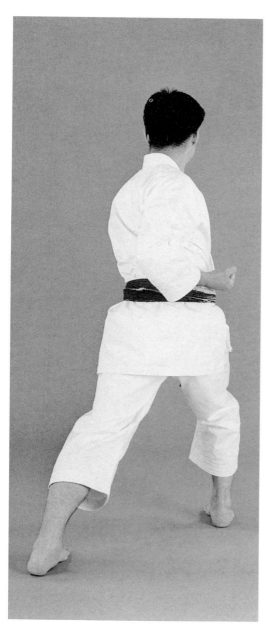

**Fig.20**

Side view

**Fig.21** Make a front snap kick with your left leg.

Side view

**Fig.22** Make a reverse punch with your right hand.

Side view

**Fig.23** *Moroteuke*. Step forward and make a block with your right hand with your left fist supporting your right elbow.

Side view

116

**Fig.23**

㉒

Side view

**㉓**

**Fig.24** Move your left foot to your left side and make a front stance downward block.

**㉔**

**Fig.25** Step 45° with your right foot and make an upper rising block with your right hand.

**Fig.26** *Above* Move your right foot to your right side and make a downward block with your right hand.

**Fig.27** *Above, right* Step 45° with your left foot and make an upper rising block with your left hand with *Kiai*.

**Fig.28** *Naore.* Step back with your left foot to ready position.

# Application

**Figs 29, 30 and 31** show the application of figs 5 to 7.

**Fig.29**

**Fig.30**

**Fig.31**

# Kumite: three-step sparring

As for Levels one and two.

# Level four (6th kyu)

## Kihon

**Fig.12** *Empi* (elbow strike). There are various ways to make an elbow strike:
**(1)** *Empi* to the side;
**(2)** *Empi* in a circular movement;
**(3)** *Empi* upwards;
**(4)** *Empi* to the rear;
**(5)** *Empi* downwards.

**(1)**

**(2)**

**(3)**

**(4)**

**(5)**

# Kata: heian sandan

**Fig.1** *Yoi* (ready).

**Fig.2** *Uchiuke*. Move your left foot to your left side and make a back stance inside block with your left hand.

❶

127

**Fig.3** Move your right foot to your left foot and make a downward block with your left hand and inside block with your right hand.                    ❷

**Fig.4** While standing in the same position, make a downward block with your ❸
right hand and inside block with your left hand.

**Fig.5** Move your right foot to the opposite direction and make a back stance inside block with your right hand.

❹

**Fig.6** Move your left foot to your right foot, and make a downward block with your right hand and inside block with your left hand. **❺**

**Fig.7** While in the same position make a downward block with your left hand and inside block with your right hand. ❻

**❼**

**Fig.8** Turn to your left and make a back stance block with your left hand, with your right hand supporting your left elbow.

**❽**

**Fig.9** Step forward to front stance. Make a downward pressing block with your left hand and spear hand strike with your right hand.

**Fig.10** *Kentsuiuchi.* Turn your right wrist anti-clockwise and at the same time pivot on your right foot and bring your left foot round to make a straddle stance and left hand hammer fist strike.

**❾**

**Fig.11** Step forward with your right foot and make a stepping punch with your right hand with *Kiai*.

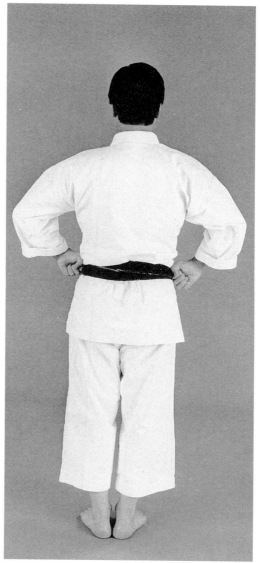

**Fig.12** Bring your left foot to your right and turn to face the opposite direction. ⑪

**Fig.13** *Fumikomi furiempi.* Make a stamping kick with your right foot.

Side view

**Fig.13**

⓬

Side view

**Fig.14** *Urakenuchi*. Make a back fist strike with your right hand.

Side view

**Fig.14**

Side view

**Fig.15** Make a stamp kick with your left foot.

Side view

Side view

**Fig.16** Make a back fist strike with your left fist.

Side view

**Fig.16**

Side view

**Fig.17** Make a stamp kick with your right foot.

Side view

**Fig.17**

Side view

**Fig.18** Make a back fist strike with your right hand.

**Fig.19** Open your right hand. At the same time shift your weight to your right leg and make a stepping punch with your left hand.

Side view

**Fig.19**

⓲

Side view

**Fig.20** Right arm: *Tsukiage;* left arm: *Empi*. Move your right foot forward and pivot on your right foot to make a straddle stance with right hand punch and left hand elbow strike to the rear.

Side view

Side view

**⑲**

**Fig.21** *Yoseashi*. Keep both feet in the same position. Slide to your right and make a left hand punch and right hand elbow strike to the rear with *Kiai*.

**Fig.21**

**Fig.22** *Naore*. Move your right foot back to ready position.

# Application

**Figs 23, 24, 25 and 26** show the application of figs 9 and 10.

**Fig.23**

**Fig.24**

**Fig.25**

**Fig.26**

# Kihon ippon kumite: one-step sparring

After bowing to each other, the attacker steps back into front stance and makes one attack to the opponent. The defender can make any block and counter attack.

One-step sparring is for Levels four, five, six and seven.

# Glossary

**PUNCHING TECHNIQUES**
**Chudan junzuki**: stepping punch to the stomach
**Empi**: elbow strike
**Gyaku zuki**: reverse punch
**Jodan junzuki**: stepping punch to the face
**Kentsuiuchi**: hammer fist strike
**Nukite**: spear hand strike
**Shutouchi**: knife hand strike
**Uraken**: back fist strike

**BLOCKING TECHNIQUES**
**Age uke**: rising block
**Gedan barai**: downward block
**Shuto uke**: knife hand block
**Soto uke**: outside block
**Uchi uke**: inside block

**KICKING TECHNIQUES**
**Mae geri**: front snap kick
**Mawashi geri**: round kick
**Ushiro geri**: back kick
**Yoko geri keage**: side snap kick
**Yoko geri kekomi**: side thrust kick

**Chudan**: stomach
**Gedan**: lower
**Jodan**: face

**STANCES**
**Kiba dachi**: straddle stance
**Kokutsu dachi**: back stance
**Zenkutsu dachi**: front stance

**Dojo**: training hall
**Gi**: karate suit
**Kata**: forms
**Keri**: kicking
**Kihon**: basic
**Kumite**: sparring
**Makiwara**: striking board
**Seiken**: fist
**Tsuki**: punching
**Uchi**: striking

# Index